# The Book of
# California Wisdom

# The Book of California Wisdom

Common Sense and Uncommon Genius
From 101 Great Californians

*Compiled and Edited by Criswell Freeman*

WALNUT GROVE PRESS
Nashville, TN
(615) 256-8584

ISBN 1-887655-14-X

*The ideas expressed in this book are not, in all cases, exact quotations, as some have been edited for clarity and brevity. In all cases, the author has attempted to maintain the speaker's original intent. In some cases, material for this book was obtained from secondary sources, primarily print media. While every effort was made to ensure the accuracy of these sources, the accuracy cannot be guaranteed. For additions, deletions, corrections or clarifications in future editions of this text, please write WALNUT GROVE PRESS.*

Printed in the United States of America
Cover Design by Mary Mazer
Typesetting & Page Layout by Sue Gerdes
Edited by Alan Ross and Angela Beasley
1 2 3 4 5 6 7 8 9 10 • 96 97 98 99 00 01

ACKNOWLEDGMENTS
The author gratefully acknowledges the helpful support of Angela Beasley, Dick and Mary Freeman, Mary Susan Freeman, and Tom Gerdes.

*For Ronny Cox*

Our Family's Favorite Movie Star

# Table of Contents

# Introduction

What America is to the world, California is to America. California, more than any other state, is the land of innovation, immigration, variation and fascination. It is a melting pot, not just of people, but of ideas.

California is also the land of "more." California boasts more people, more industry, more cars, and, if it could be measured, more dreams than any of her sister states. The forty-niner spirit still lives.

The genius of California springs from its diversity and its intensity. This book chronicles the wisdom, humor and inspiration of 101 notable Californians along with the insights of a few guests, sight-seers and tourists.

From Jerry Garcia to Jerry Brown, from William Saroyan to Willie Mays, Californians have much to say. And the rest of the world, it seems, is more than happy to listen. The men and women on these pages prove that there is much more to the Golden State than tinsel and surfboards. Although California is America's fantasy land, the wisdom of her sons and daughters is very real indeed.

# 1

## California

In 1967, the *American Guide Series* concluded, "Now more than ever before, California is the rainbow's end for great numbers of Americans." Today, these words still apply, only more so. The Golden State has become the rainbow's end not just for Americans but also for a great number of the world's citizens.

Why has the rush to California continued, largely unabated, since gold was discovered at Sutter's Mill? Because California seemingly has everything. It boasts a breathtakingly diverse geography and a dynamic economy. It sets trends and creates dreams. The world keeps a watchful eye on California, and California doesn't disappoint.

The following quotations pay tribute to the Golden State. The rainbow stops here.

California, the most spectacular and most diversified American state — California so ripe, golden, yeasty, churning in a flux, is a world of its own.

*John Gunther*

Californians are
a race of people;
they are not merely
inhabitants of a state.

*O. Henry*

*California*

California, more than any other part
of the Union, is a country by itself,
and San Francisco is the capital.

*James Bryce, 1901*


There are several Californias.
The state is at once demented and very sane,
adolescent and mature, depending
on the point of view.

*John Gunther*


California, since we took it from the Mexicans,
has always presented itself to Americans
as one of the strangest and most exotic
of their exploits.

*Edmund Wilson*


People come to California, I say,
to get out of the world.

*Harrison Salisbury*

There is no part of earth here where there is
not some special likelihood of gold or silver.
*Richard Hakluyt, 1589*

The whole country from San Francisco
to Los Angeles and from sea shore
to the base of the Sierra Nevada
resounds with the sordid cry of gold!
Gold! Gold!!
*The Californian, 1850*

One of the most alluring things about
Southern California is the image in the minds
of its people of what this land can be.
*Neil Morgan*

Southern California has completely bowled
me over — such a delicious difference
from the rest of the United States.

*Henry James, 1905*

The important thing to know about
Southern California is that the people who
live here, who grew up here, love it.
Not just the way one has an attachment
to a hometown, any hometown, but the way
people love the realization that they
have found the right mode of life.

*James Q. Wilson*

California, in a way, has turned its back
on the world, and looks into
the void of the Pacific.

*D. H. Lawrence, 1923*

California is the department store state.

*Raymond Chandler*

All scenery in California requires distance
to give it its highest charm.

*Mark Twain, 1872*

As for the people in California,
they are samples of all our people.
They come from every state to enjoy
climate and scenery.

*Pearl S. Buck*

I attended a dinner given
for the Old Settlers
of California. No one was
allowed to attend unless
he had been in the state
two and one-half years.

*Will Rogers*

# 2

# Nature

Naturalist John Muir was a founding member of the Sierra Club. It is no surprise that he treasured the mountain range that gave the club its name. Muir described the Sierras as having, "the brightest weather, the brightest glacier-polished rocks, glorious waterfalls, the brightest forests of silver firs and silver pines, more star shine and moonshine, and perhaps more crystal shine than any other mountain chain."

One of Muir's contemporaries was Luther Burbank, a horticulturist who moved to Santa Rosa in 1875. Burbank noted, "Nature's laws affirm instead of prohibit. If you violate her laws, you are your own prosecuting attorney, judge, jury and hangman."

On the pages that follow, we celebrate the natural wonders of John Muir's Golden State. But the job of protecting California's natural beauty is never finished. As Luther Burbank correctly observed, Mother Nature is always watching.

*Nature*

California could be a dozen states,
    each with its own outdoor personality,
    its own climate, its own natural wonders.
                                        *Insight Guides*

The various landscapes of California —
    it is Switzerland and Burgundy and
    Yorkshire and Scotland and Spain.
                                        *Alistair Cooke*

The flashing and golden pageant of California,
    the sudden and gorgeous drama,
    the sunny and ample lands.
                                        *Walt Whitman*

California has better days, and more of them,
    than any other country.
                                *Ralph Waldo Emerson, 1871*

For all of California's sweetness and
    artificiality, the primordial cycles of fire
    and rain and earthquake continue,
    nature keeping man in his place.
                                        *Neal R. Peirce*

This slender ribbon of land and water
is remarkable in many ways; its variety,
its climate, its promise.

*Merrill Windsor*

The spring is beautiful in California.
Valleys are filled with fruit blossoms that are
fragrant pink. Then, the first tendrils of the
grapes swelling from the old gnarled vines
cascade down to cover the trunks.

*John Steinbeck, 1939*

The climate is, according to the Californians,
perennial spring. But eulogy in this direction
reached its acme when an enthusiastic writer
declared the climate of California to be
eminently favourable to the cure
of gunshot wounds.

*G. A. Sala, 1882*

*Nature*

The Pacific coast in general is the paradise
of conifers. Here, nearly all of them are giants.

*John Muir, 1911*


When a tree takes a notion to grow
in California nothing in heaven or earth
will stop it.

*Lilian Leland, 1890*


Give me men to match my mountains.

*Inscribed on the State Capitol, Sacramento*


I know no single wonder on earth which
can claim a superiority over Yosemite.

*Horace Greeley*


Nature has endowed the north of California
with resources that will endure and flourish
when Hollywood has disappeared into the
prehistoric tarpits of Wilshire Boulevard.

*Charlie Chaplin, 1910*

I thought Lake Tahoe must surely be
the finest picture the whole earth affords.

*Mark Twain*

Santa Rosa — the chosen spot on earth.

*Luther Burbank*

Within the rock wall formed by California's
two great mountain ranges lies the
Sacramento-San Joaquin or Central Valley.
It has been called the world's
most fertile growing region.

*American Guide Series*

Every day of my life at Big Sur I had
   before me the incomparable vista of the
Pacific. Its ever-changing aspects offered me
   alternately peace and stimulation.

*Henry Miller*

Big Sur is a state of mind.

*Reader's Digest, 1973*

Big Sur is the face of the earth
   as the creator intended it to look.

*Henry Miller*

The Mojave is a big desert and a frightening
one. It's as though nature tested a man for
endurance and constancy to prove whether
he was good enough to get to California.

*John Steinbeck*

Its beauty and its Mediterranean climate
have made southern California one of the
most heavily populated spots in the world.

*Bill Thomas*

# Let children walk with Nature.

*John Muir*

# 3

# Change

California is trend-setter to the world. In the Golden State, change is as inevitable as sunshine. Dream-maker Walt Disney understood the profound power of new ideas and consciously avoided the temptation to copy himself.

After the success of *The Three Little Pigs* in 1933, theater owners clamored for a sequel. The message to Disney was clear: "More pigs!" But Walt, in his wisdom, declined. He said simply, "You can't top pigs with pigs."

When the Greek philosopher Heraclitus observed, "Nothing endures but change," he could have been speaking directly to Californians. No matter how much we protest, the world continues to change, and if we're smart, we change right along with it.

Whatever starts in California
has an inclination to spread.

*Jimmy Carter*

California, the advance post
of our civilization.

*J. B. Priestley*

Peter's Law: The unexpected always happens.

*Laurence J. Peter*

All adventures, especially into new territory,
are scary.

*Sally Ride*

Almost anything might
work in California,
so you never know.

*Carey McWilliams*

The significant tense for human beings is
the future tense.

*Rollo May*

Either you sacrifice for the future,
or you steal from it.

*Jerry Brown*

The future: that period of time in which
our affairs prosper, our friends are true, and
our happiness is assured.

*Ambrose Bierce*

Never make predictions,
especially about the future.

*Sam Goldwyn*

Change is happening all the time,
and it's okay.

*Jerry Garcia*

Total security has never been available
to anyone. To expect it is unrealistic. To
imagine that it can exist is to invite disaster.

*Edward Teller*

Even in slight things, the experience
of the new is rarely without some stirring
of foreboding.

*Eric Hoffer*

It is the nature of man as he grows older
to protest against change, particularly
for the better.

*John Steinbeck*

It takes guts to leave the ruts.

*Robert Schuller*

*Change*

It is best for thinking people to change
their minds occasionally in order to keep
them clean. For those who do not think,
it is best at least to rearrange
their prejudices once in a while.

*Luther Burbank*

Nothing should be permanent except the
struggle against the dark side
within ourselves.

*Shirley MacLaine*

Anytime anybody tells me the trend
is such and such, I do the opposite.

*Clint Eastwood*

If everyone is thinking alike,
then somebody is not thinking.

*George S. Patton*

No one changes the world
who isn't obsessed.

*Billie Jean King*

We used to think that revolutions
are the cause of change. Actually, it's the
other way around: Change prepares
the ground for revolution.

*Eric Hoffer*

Men do change.

*John Steinbeck*

Tomorrow comes to us at midnight
very clean. It's perfect when it arrives,
and it puts itself in our hands and hopes
we've learnt something for yesterday.

*John Wayne*

In modern society,
the opposite of courage
is not cowardice;
it is conformity.

*Rollo May*

# 4

# Happiness

One of Walt Disney's notable television discoveries was guitarist Jimmie Dodd, adult host of *The Mickey Mouse Club*. Jimmie, the pure essence of kindness and wisdom, never hesitated to share an aphorism with his youthful audience. As Dodd once observed, "Proverbs help us all become better Mouseketeers."

On the following pages, notable Californians share lessons about happiness. Why? Because they like you!

Happiness is a matter of your own doing.
You can be happy or you can be unhappy.
It's just according to the way
you look at things.

*Walt Disney*

If I have the power to create unhappiness,
I also have the power to uncreate it.

*Shirley MacLaine*

I'm happier because I made up my mind
to be that way.

*Merle Haggard*

Misery is a bad choice.

*William Glasser*

The world is as good
as you are. You've got
to learn to like
yourself first.

*Steve McQueen*

The perfect day?
If you wake up and you're not in the obituaries,
it's a good start.

*Johnny Carson*

Happiness makes up in height for what
it lacks in length.

*Robert Frost*

The secret to happiness is being yourself.

*Dan Blocker*

Happiness means quiet nerves.

*W. C. Fields*

As long as I can work, I'm happy.

*Lucille Ball*

You have freedom when you're
easy in the harness.

*Robert Frost*

Some things in life you just can't buy —
like great memories.

*Don Drysdale*

Too much of a good thing can be wonderful.

*Mae West*

Happiness is not a question of having
or not having problems.

*Robert Schuller*

Remembering the good times
gets you through the bad times.

*Walter Alston*

I've learned you're no happier in big houses
than you are in modest ones.

*Michael Landon*

We can never have enough of that
which we really do not want.

*Eric Hoffer*

Don't go out looking for happiness.
Happiness is a by-product.

*Johnny Carson*

The search for happiness is one
of the chief sources of unhappiness.

*Eric Hoffer*

The greatest happiness you can have
is knowing that you do not necessarily
require happiness.

*William Saroyan*

# Hollywood is where, if you don't have happiness, you send out for it.

*Rex Reed*

Happiness is having
a large, caring, close-knit
family in another city.

*George Burns*

*Happiness*

I love my work, but work itself
        doesn't add up to happiness.
        Happiness is sharing a life.

*Michael Landon*

It is so important to have what I call
        the enchanted sense of play.

*Lucille Ball*

A sad soul can kill you quicker than a germ.

*John Steinbeck*

Play happy.

*Willie Mays*

# 5

# All-Purpose Advice

John Steinbeck was born in Salinas. After specializing in marine biology at Stanford, Steinbeck began writing. Great acclaim followed, culminating in 1962 when he was awarded the Nobel Prize for Literature. Steinbeck wrote, "No one wants advice — only corroboration." With apologies to those who seek only confirmation, this chapter contains a wide assortment of Golden State wisdom.

Love yourself first.

*Lucille Ball*

Try and live your life the way you wish
other people would live theirs.

*Raymond Burr*

Seek goodness everywhere.

*William Saroyan*

As earthlings, it's best for us
to stick together.

*Jerry Garcia*

# Make each day your masterpiece.

*John Wooden*

Time given to thought is
    the greatest time saver of all.

*Norman Cousins*


The best way to have a good idea
    is to have lots of ideas.

*Linus Pauling*


It's unfulfilled dreams that keep you alive.

*Robert Schuller*


Take calculated risks. That is quite different
    from being rash.

*George S. Patton*


Don't retire.

*George Burns*

Learn to cook. That's the way
to save money!

*Julia Child*

Spare no expense to make everything
as economical as possible.

*Sam Goldwyn*

A verbal contract isn't worth the paper
it's written on.

*Sam Goldwyn*

Tear up the standard contract
and write your own.

*Jerry Garcia*

Be more concerned with your character
than your reputation. Your character is what
you really are, while your reputation is
merely what others think you are.

*John Wooden*

I never wanted to adopt a mask.
I feared my face would grow into it.

*Shirley MacLaine*

Don't compromise yourself.
You are all you've got.

*Janis Joplin*

The most important part of managing?
Be yourself.

*Walter Alston*

Climb the mountains and get their good
tidings. Nature's peace will flow into you as
sunshine flows into trees.

*John Muir*

I've always followed my father's advice.
He told me, first, to always keep my word;
second, to never insult anybody intentionally;
and, third, not to go around
looking for trouble.

*John Wayne*

Talk low, talk slow, and don't say too much.

*John Wayne*

Do your best and forget the rest.

*Walter Alston*

# Never make fun of religion, politics, race or mothers.

*Mack Sennett*

Don't offer advice to your kids
unless they ask for it.

*Ozzie Nelson*

Never tell people how to do things.
Tell them what to do, and they will surprise
you with their ingenuity.

*George S. Patton*

The best advice may be no advice.
That's not my line. It's from a fortune cookie.

*George Burns*

# Remember Lot's wife. Never look back.

*Richard M. Nixon*

# 6

# Attitude

Tom Bradley overcame very long odds to become Los Angeles' first African-American mayor. How did Mayor Bradley explain success? He once commented, "Attitude is a person's most important asset."

A healthy outlook can never be taxed or stolen, but it can be shared. On the following pages, savvy Californians contribute their insights about an asset that costs nothing yet pays enormous dividends: a positive mental attitude.

Don't believe in pessimism.

*Clint Eastwood*

Pessimism is a mental disease.

*Upton Sinclair*

One of the things I learned the hard way
was that it doesn't pay to get discouraged.
Keeping busy and making optimism a way
of life can restore your faith in yourself.

*Lucille Ball*

In the presence of hope, faith is born.

*Robert Schuller*

Entertain great hopes.

*Robert Frost*

There is a giant asleep
in every man. When
that giant wakes,
miracles happen.

*Frederick Faust*

# If you can dream it, you can do it.

*Walt Disney*

The only thing that will stop you from fulfilling your dream is you.

*Tom Bradley*

*Attitude*

Nobody becomes great without self-doubt,
but you can't let it control you.

*John McKay*

You always have to believe in yourself
before others can believe in you.

*Tommy Lasorda*

Courage is fear holding on a minute longer.

*George S. Patton*

The tougher the fight, the more important
the mental attitude.

*Michael Landon*

Peace is not made at the council tables,
but in the hearts of men.

*Herbert Hoover*


While I would not have missed yesterday,
I have no desire to go back and live it over.
For me, there is only the great today,
and the promise of tomorrow.

*Mary Pickford*


I don't like looking back.
I'm looking ahead to the next show.
It's how I keep young.

*Jack Benny*


Success is never final. Failure is never fatal.
It's courage that counts.

*John Wooden*

*Attitude*

I've never been poor, only broke.
Being poor is a frame of mind. Being broke
is only a temporary situation.

*Mike Todd*


Assume responsibility for the quality
of your own life.

*Norman Cousins*


If the will remains in protest,
it stays dependent on that which
it is protesting against.

*Rollo May*


You are not the physical or psychological
slave of your parents, husband, wife, child,
boss, the economy, or anything else —
unless you choose to be.

*William Glasser*

The difference between the possible
and the impossible lies in
a person's determination.

*Tommy Lasorda*

You have to believe in yourself.
That's the secret.

*Charlie Chaplin*

You are the architect of your own experience.

*Shirley MacLaine*

If you think it's going to rain, it will.

*Clint Eastwood*

Some criticism will be honest, some won't.
Some praise you will deserve, some you
won't. You can't let praise or criticism
get to you. It's a weakness to get
caught up in either one.

*John Wooden*

If your self-esteem rests upon social
validation, you have not self-esteem,
but a more sophisticated form
of social conformity.

*Rollo May*

Hope is desire and expectation
rolled into one.

*Ambrose Bierce*

We are told that talent creates its own
opportunities. But it sometimes seems
that intense desire creates not only its
own opportunities, but its own talents.

*Eric Hoffer*

There is no terror in a bang,
only the anticipation of it.

*Alfred Hitchcock*

All men are afraid in battle.
The coward is the one who lets his fear
overcome his sense of duty.

*George S. Patton*

Fear corrupts.

*John Steinbeck*

Love what's lovable
and hate what's hateable.

*Robert Frost*

The person who knows
how to laugh at himself
will never cease
to be amused.

*Shirley MacLaine*

# 7

# Adversity

Perhaps no Californian ever faced more public indignity than Richard Nixon. As the nation watched, President Nixon's world crumbled around him; eventually he resigned in disgrace.

During his White House farewell, a shaken Mr. Nixon spoke these words: "Always remember others may hate you, but those who hate you don't win unless you hate them back. And then you destroy yourself." Miraculously, Nixon did not destroy himself. Instead, he fought the good fight, continued to contribute, and persevered until the last.

Few of us will ever experience the public ignominy that confronted Richard Nixon in 1974. Still, each of us must learn our own lessons about hardship. Adversity is the price that the world occasionally extracts in exchange for the precious gift of life. On the following pages, notable Californians teach us lessons that were learned and earned the hard way: at the school of hard knocks.

There can be no real freedom
without the freedom to fail.

*Eric Hoffer*

When do you develop character?
After you've learned to survive defeat.

*Richard M. Nixon*

You always pass failure
on the way to success.

*Mickey Rooney*

The road to Easy Street
goes through the sewer.

*John Madden*

You must come to grips with misfortune
and go on.

*Shirley Temple Black*

How to survive tragedy?
Throw yourself into work, work, work.

*Raymond Burr*

Supposing you have tried and failed
again and again. You have a fresh start
any moment you choose, for this thing
we call "failure" is not the falling down,
but the staying down.

*Mary Pickford*

The finest steel has to go through
the hottest fire.

*Richard M. Nixon*

Learn from your mistakes.
Don't beat your head against the same
mistakes over and over.

*Lucille Ball*

Until we lose ourselves, there is no hope
of finding ourselves.

*Henry Miller*

Good people are good because they've
come to wisdom through failure.

*William Saroyan*

I always thought it mattered to know
what is the worst possible thing that can
happen to you, to know how you can avoid it,
to not be drawn by the magic
of the unspeakable.

*Amy Tan*


Words are less needful to sorrow than joy.

*Helen Hunt Jackson*


Problems are only opportunities
in work clothes.

*Henry J. Kaiser*


Never look at what you have lost.
Look at what you have left.

*Robert Schuller*

Notice the difference between
what happens when a man says to himself,
"I have failed three times," and what happens
when he says, "I am a failure."

*S. I. Hayakawa*

When you can't solve the problem,
manage it.

*Robert Schuller*

When a man is finally boxed in,
and he has no choice, he begins
to decorate his box.

*John Steinbeck*

For every peak, there's a valley,
        so don't get too high.

*John Wooden*


Look at misfortune the same way
        you look at success. Don't panic.

*Walter Alston*

A problem difficult at night is often resolved in the morning after the committee of sleep has worked on it.

*John Steinbeck*

# Don't let what you cannot do interfere with what you can do.

*John Wooden*

Tough times never last,
but tough people do.

*Robert Schuller*

# 8

# Other People

Fresno-born William Saroyan spent his childhood in the presence of Armenian immigrants and farmers. Shortly after leaving school at age fifteen, William began writing short stories. Within a decade, his considerable literary skills were evident.

Saroyan once noted, "Every man in the world is better than someone else. And not as good as someone else." On the following pages, noteworthy Californians consider the ethical treatment of others. William Saroyan identified the proper starting point for improved human relations: the understanding that, in the end, we are more alike than we imagine.

Love has a tide.

*Helen Hunt Jackson*

Life is an exercise in forgiveness.

*Norman Cousins*

Love is my decision to make your problem
my problem.

*Robert Schuller*

When you make someone laugh,
you're giving him medicine.

*Danny Kaye*

Love conquers all things except poverty
and a tooth ache.

*Mae West*

I never hated a man enough to give him
his diamonds back.

*Zsa Zsa Gabor*

*Other People*

Be decent and fair. But ultimately,
you have to know how to get the work done
whether or not people like you for it.

*Sally Field*

Most serious conflicts evolve
from our attempts to control others
who will not accept our control.

*William Glasser*

If you isolate your problem from others,
your chances of solving it are thin.
Problems require wisdom, and wisdom
requires perspective. Other people
provide that perspective.

*Bill Russell*

It's amazing how much can be accomplished
if no one cares who gets the credit.

*John Wooden*

We destroy people by creating within them
a state of permanent dependency.

*S. I. Hayakawa*

A word can be a balm or a bomb,
so make your words positive.

*Robert Schuller*

We are made kind by being kind.

*Eric Hoffer*

You can't fake listening.

*Raquel Welch*

To improve communications, work not on
the utterer, but on the recipient.

*Peter Drucker*

The more I traveled, the more I realized
that fear makes strangers of people
who should be friends.

*Shirley MacLaine*

Criticism is more than what we say;
it is also a way of looking at other people
with disdain.

*William Glasser*

The less secure a man is, the more likely
he is to have extreme prejudice.

*Clint Eastwood*

Rudeness is the weak man's
imitation of strength.

*Eric Hoffer*

When someone
does something good,
applaud! You'll make
two people happy.

*Sam Goldwyn*

If something comes to life in others because of you, then you have made an approach to immortality.

*Norman Cousins*

# 9

## Action

The Gold Rush of 1848 brought a horde of dreamers and schemers to Northern California. In typical Golden State fashion, the hype was intense. A forty-niner named Jesse Hutchinson penned these words:

*Then, ho, brothers, ho*
*To California go;*
*There's plenty of gold in the world we're told*
*On the banks of the Sacramento.*

Unfortunately for Hutchinson and his compatriots, the gold mania soon ran its course, and the speculators went bust. But a swaggering attitude remained.

Californians don't wait for things to happen; they make things happen. If natives of the Golden State seem propelled by a powerful mixture of hope and energy, it's no surprise. Energetic optimism is a state tradition.

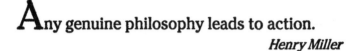

*Action*

$A$ny genuine philosophy leads to action.
*Henry Miller*

$W$ords without actions are the assassins
of idealism.
*Herbert Hoover*

$O$ne who doesn't try cannot fail
and become wise.
*William Saroyan*

$Y$ou ought to take the bull between the teeth.
*Sam Goldwyn*

Inaction may be the
highest form of action.

*Jerry Brown*

*Action*

If you cease to be ready to face
the frightening, then you become old.

*S. I. Hayakawa*

If you take no risks, you suffer no defeats.
But if you take no risks, you will win
no victories.

*Richard M. Nixon*

An individuals's life is constituted
by his or her choices.

*Irvin Yalom*

Every new adjustment is a crisis
in self-esteem.

*Eric Hoffer*

Again and again
the impossible problem
is solved when we see
that the problem is
only a tough decision
waiting to be made.

*Robert Schuller*

To dispose a soul to action we must upset
its equilibrium.

*Eric Hoffer*

In war, nothing is impossible,
provided you use audacity.

*George S. Patton*

Act quickly but don't hurry.

*John Wooden*

There is nothing so useless
as doing efficiently that which
should not be done at all.

*Peter Drucker*

The best way out is always through.

*Robert Frost*

If you really want something,
you can figure out how to make it happen.

*Cher*

Luck is the sense to recognize
an opportunity and the ability
to take advantage of it.

*Sam Goldwyn*

Eureka!

*State Motto*

Whenever you see
a successful business,
someone once made a
courageous decision.

*Peter Drucker*

All our dreams can
come true if we
have the courage
to pursue them.

*Walt Disney*

How can you say
luck and chance are
the same things?
Chance is the first step
you take, luck is what
comes afterwards.

*Amy Tan*

# 10

## Success

Situated on a Malibu cliff, the J. Paul Getty Museum overlooks the Pacific. Its benefactor, the late Mr. Getty, was once considered the world's richest man.

Getty inherited a fortune and then multiplied it many times over in the oil fields. In just six words, he summed up his formula for success: "Rise early. Work late. Strike oil!"

By most accounts, J. Paul Getty's personal life was not a particularly joyful one. He was married five times and, in later years, became infamous for his miserly ways. Getty earned a spot in the humbug's hall of fame when he installed a pay-phone in his own home for the use of his guests. So much for the milk of human kindness.

Mr. Getty proved that success is not denominated in dollars and cents. As you read the quotations that follow, take a moment to examine your own life. Define exactly what success means to you and create a success formula of your own.

Success is not a harbor but a voyage.

*Richard M. Nixon*

I don't want winners. I want champions.

*Jerry Buss*

You can make all the money you want,
but there's nothing like winning.

*Tony Gwynn*

Ability may get you to the top,
but it takes character to keep you there.

*John Wooden*

The Book of California Wisdom

Success is talent, hard work and luck.

*Kareem Abdul-Jabbar*

You have to be at the right place
at the right time. But then you
have to be ready.

*Johnny Carson*

You've got to be lucky, but then you've got
to be able to take advantage of your luck.

*Chuck Conners*

The best things in movies
happen by accident.

*John Ford*

$G$et a good idea and stay with it,
and work it until it's done and done right.

*Walt Disney*


$I$t's not what you do once in a while;
it's what you do day in and out
that makes the difference.

*Jenny Craig*


$W$hen you fight for a desperate cause
and have good reason to fight,
you usually win.

*Edward Teller*

Work for quality, not quantity
or quick money.

*Walt Disney*

Quality is not what the supplier puts in —
it's what the customer gets out.

*Peter Drucker*

We go to every length we can to insure
quality all along the line.

*Jerry Garcia*

Failure is never final
and success is never-ending.

*Robert Schuller*

*Success*

The only thing harder to handle
than winning too much is losing too much.

*John Wooden*

Perhaps the truest axiom is
that the toughest thing to do is repeat.
The tendency is to relax
without even knowing it.

*Walter Alston*

The only problem with doing the impossible
is that everybody expects you
to duplicate the impossible.

*John McKay*

A man is not finished when he is defeated.
He is finished when he quits.

*Richard M. Nixon*

It is the picture of success in *your* head,
nobody else's, that causes you to do
what you do.

*William Glasser*

If you don't know where you're going,
you will probably end up somewhere else.

*Laurence J. Peter*

Don't measure yourself by what you have
accomplished but by what you should have
accomplished with your ability.

*John Wooden*

Surround yourself with the best people;
delegate authority; and as long as your policy
is carried out, don't interfere.

*Ronald Reagan*

It is better to attempt something great
and fail than to attempt nothing and succeed.

*Robert Schuller*

Success is energy.

*Fay Dunaway*

Do everything.
One thing may turn out right.

*Humphrey Bogart*

Success is being truly happy at what you do.

*Tommy Lasorda*

Movie stars to the south; majestic solitude
to the north. Can you blame anyone
for thinking California was his best
possible chance for success?

*Insight Guides*

It's great to be involved in something that
doesn't hurt anybody. If it provides
some comfort in people's lives,
it's just that much nicer.

*Jerry Garcia*

You can keep the things of bronze and stone
and give me one man to remember me
just once a year.

*Damon Runyon*

No endeavor that is worthwhile is simple in prospect. But, if it is right, it will be simple in retrospect.

*Edward Teller*

# 11

## Hard Work

UCLA had a mediocre basketball program until 1948, the year the school hired a young coach named John Wooden. Wooden immediately installed a disciplined, high-pressure running attack. Before he was through, his Bruins won ten national championships.

Wooden-coached teams were renowned for their mental preparation and physical conditioning. Allowing no slackers, Coach Wooden observed, "My definition of success is peace of mind obtained by doing the best you can to be the best you are."

Through hard work, potential is transformed into reality. For more thoughts on the transformation process, turn the page.

*Hard Work*

I'd rather make $200 a week
doing something I love than a million dollars
doing something I hate.

*George Burns*

The world doesn't owe you a living.
Nothing is more important than being able
to stand on your own two feet.

*Lucille Ball*

Never continue in a job you don't enjoy.
If you're happy in what you're doing,
you'll like yourself, and that's success.

*Johnny Carson*

I dream for a living.

*Steven Spielberg*

My best advice?
Fall in love with what
you do for a living.

*George Burns*

$F$ailure to prepare is preparing to fail.

*John Wooden*

$T$he reason that worry kills more people
than work is that more people worry
than work.

*Robert Frost*

$T$he better we understand ourselves,
the better we are at our work.

*Shirley MacLaine*

$W$hen your work speaks for itself,
don't interrupt.

*Henry J. Kaiser*

The only way to enjoy anything in this life
is to earn it first.

*Ginger Rogers*

Luck is hard work and realizing what
opportunity is — and what it isn't.

*Lucille Ball*

Attempt the impossible in order
to improve your work.

*Bette Davis*

Nothing will work unless you do.

*John Wooden*

## Hard Work

I don't deal with yesterday,
and I don't wait for tomorrow. I deal with
today with as much energy as I can summon.
*Jack Nicholson*


Learn to take your work seriously
and not yourself seriously.
*Clint Eastwood*


To fulfill a dream, to be allowed to sweat
over lonely labor, to be given a chance
to create — this is the meat and potatoes
of life. Money is the gravy.
*Bette Davis*


Work hard and go home happy.
*Michael Landon*


Age to me means nothing.
I can't get old — I'm working.
*George Burns*

One's trek through life
is limited only by oneself
and one's willingness
to work.

*Ginger Rogers*

No person who
is enthusiastic about
his work has anything
to fear from life.

*Sam Goldwyn*

# 12

## Life

Life presents each of us with a perplexing challenge: How do we grow up without growing old? Anthropologist Ashley Montagu once wrote, "In other parts of the world, youth lasts a reasonable period of time; in California, it lasts a lifetime."

On the pages that follow, Californians share their secrets.

Life itself is the proper binge.

*Julia Child*

A happy life is spent learning
and earning and yearning.

*Lillian Gish*

Life, for everyone, is a series of crises.

*Richard M. Nixon*

In life, all good things come hard,
but wisdom is the hardest to come by.

*Lucille Ball*

# Always be in a state of becoming.

*Walt Disney*

# In the time of your life, live.

*William Saroyan*

The man who limits his interests
limits his life.

*Vincent Price*

The days in my life that stand out most
vividly are the days I've learned something.
Learning is so exciting I get goose bumps.

*Lucille Ball*

Life is a great big canvas, and you
should throw all the paint on it you can.

*Danny Kaye*

Be. Live. And don't worry too much
about the troubles that loom so large today.
They will pass.

*Mickey Rooney*

In three words I can sum up everything
I've learned about life: It goes on.

*Robert Frost*

*Life*

The trick to life, I can now say
in my advanced age, is to stop trying
to make it so important.

*Loretta Young*


Life is for each man a solitary cell
whose walls are mirrors.

*Eugene O'Neill*


Life is tragedy when seen in close-up,
but comedy in long-shot.

*Charlie Chaplin*


There is only one thing age can give you,
and that's wisdom.

*S. I. Hayakawa*


What makes life worth something
is purpose, a goal, the battle, the struggle —
even if you don't win it.

*Richard M. Nixon*

Man's loneliness is but his fear of life.

*Eugene O'Neill*

Timing is the essence of life.

*Bob Hope*

The very commonplaces of life
are components of its eternal mystery.

*Gertrude Atherton*

I don't want life to imitate art.
I want life to be art.

*Carrie Fisher*

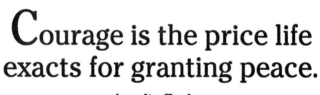

Courage is the price life
exacts for granting peace.

*Amelia Earhart*

Man is a stubborn seeker of meaning.
*John Gardner*

Selfishness turns life into a burden.
Unselfishness turns burdens into life!
*Robert Schuller*

In the end, life must be what you do with
yourself. It is working to the consummation
of your own identity.
*Shirley MacLaine*

It is not true that we have only one life
to live. If we can read, we can live as many
lives and as many kinds of lives as we wish.
*S. I. Hayakawa*

Death is not the greatest loss in life.
The greatest loss is what dies inside us
while we live.

*Norman Cousins*

Death is the fact which makes the present
hour something of absolute value.

*Rollo May*

Right from the start, we are dying.
Live to the limit every minute of every day.
Whatever you want to do, do it now.

*Michael Landon*

You're never too old to become younger.

*Mae West*

A man is not old
until regrets take
the place of dreams.

*John Barrymore*

You know you're getting old
when the candles cost more than the cake.
*Bob Hope*

Age is strictly a case of mind over matter.
If you don't mind, it doesn't matter.
*Jack Benny*

Old age is like everything else.
To make a success of it,
you've got to start young.
*Fred Astaire*

It's not how old you are, but how you are old.
*Marie Dressler*

A man, after he has brushed off the dust
and chips of his life, will have left only
the hard, clean question: Was it good
or was it evil? Have I done well or ill?

*John Steinbeck*

Prancing around on stage
is not the entire purpose of life.

*Grace Slick*

If life were fair, Elvis would be alive
and all the impersonators would be dead.

*Johnny Carson*

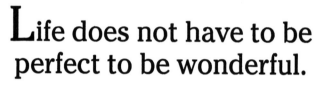

Life does not have to be perfect to be wonderful.

*Annette Funicello*

# 13

## San Francisco and Los Angeles

This chapter examines two very different places: San Francisco and Los Angeles. California boasts many wonderful cities and towns, but these two have captured the world's imagination.

San Francisco, the unofficial capital of Northern California, has more history. Of the two, it is the big sister. Los Angeles, the hub of Southern California, is the brash younger sibling intent upon upstaging everyone else in the family. For interesting insights into California's unconventional sister cities, read on.

*San Francisco and Los Angeles*

This straggling town, San Francisco,
shall become a vast metropolis; this sparsely
populated land shall become a crowded hive
of busy men.

*Mark Twain, 1866*


Of course, San Francisco has always been a
gambling city. It is in the marrow and braincells
of her people, whether their blood ancestors
were "forty-niners" or not.

*Gertrude Atherton, 1889*


San Francisco was New York with
no New England on one side of it and
no shrewd and orderly rural population
on the other to keep it in order.

*James Bryce, 1889*


When I was a child growing up in Salinas,
we called San Francisco 'the City.' Of course,
it was the only city we knew, but I still think of
it as the City, and so does everyone else
who has ever associated with it.

*John Steinbeck, 1962*

San Francisco is the lightest-hearted, most
pleasure-loving city in the Western continent.

*Will Irwin*

San Francisco is the cool grey city of love.

*George Sterling*

In San Francisco there is the best Chinese
settlement in the western world.

*Pearl S. Buck*

San Francisco is not part of America.

*Bill Graham*

Well, it hasn't taken long to fall in love
with San Francisco.

*T. H. White*

San Francisco is a mad city inhabited
by perfectly insane people whose women
are of remarkable beauty.

*Rudyard Kipling*

San Francisco: a cosmopolitan labyrinth
of intimate surprises.

*Barnaby Conrad*

San Francisco is a city with eleven months
and several odd days of Indian Summer.

*Charles Groves*

In San Francisco, we get baseball weather
in football season and football weather
in July and August.

*Herb Caen*

San Francisco is the happiest city
we have visited.

*T. H. White*

San Francisco has only
one drawback.
'Tis hard to leave.

*Rudyard Kipling, 1988*

Los Angeles is a circus without a tent.
*Carey McWilliams, 1946*

Los Angeles:
Nineteen suburbs in search of a metropolis.
*H. L. Mencken, 1925*

Los Angeles is my favorite museum.
*David Bowie*

No city in this hemisphere
has a more varied natural environment
within a few hours' drive than Los Angeles.
*Bill Thomas*

If you tilt the whole country sideways, Los Angeles is the place where everything loose will fall.

*Frank Lloyd Wright*

On Venice Beach I once saw a man blowing
truly spectacular soap bubbles the size of
watermelons. This is the symbol for me of the
tendency of people in Southern California
to become awfully good at something
that isn't terribly important.

*Calvin Trillin*

If you live in Beverly Hills they don't put
blinkers in your car. They figure if you're
that rich you don't have to tell people
where you're going.

*Bette Midler*

Beverly Hills is so exclusive even
the fire department won't make house calls.

*Woody Allen*

Strip the phoney tinsel
off Hollywood and you'll
find the real tinsel
underneath.

*Oscar Levant*

Hollywood is a carnival
where there are no concessions.

*Wilson Mizner*

No one ever really leaves Hollywood unless
they are called away by God. Even then, the
impulse would be to come back again and
make a movie about the experience.

*Shirley MacLaine*

# 14

## Observations on Movies, Politics, and Other California Necessities

We conclude with a potpourri of wisdom from the Golden State. Enjoy.

Minor surgery is when they do
the operation on someone else.

*Bill Walton*

My doctor told me I had the heart of a lion,
so I got a second opinion
from my veterinarian.

*George Burns*

I am disturbed when I see a cigarette
between the lips of some important person
upon whose intelligence and judgment
the world in part depends.

*Linus Pauling*

Pictures are for entertainment.
Messages should be delivered
by Western Union.

*Sam Goldwyn*

Our comedies are not to be laughed at.

*Sam Goldwyn*

I don't want any "yes-men" around me.
I want everybody to tell me the truth,
even if it costs them their jobs.

*Sam Goldwyn*

What the world needs is some new clichés.

*Sam Goldwyn*

Include me out.

*Sam Goldwyn*

*Observations*

The only sure thing about luck
is that it will change.

*Bret Harte*

The race is not always to the swift
nor the battle to the strong,
but that's the best way to bet.

*Damon Runyon*

Today, if you build a better mousetrap,
the government comes along
with a better mouse.

*Ronald Reagan*

A lawsuit is a machine you go into as a pig
and come out as a sausage.

*Ambrose Bierce*

A bank is a place that will lend you money
if you can prove you don't need it.

*Bob Hope*

Communication is in the ear
of the beholder.

*Tom Hayden*

A bore is a person who talks
when you want him to listen.

*Ambrose Bierce*

A bore is a person who can change
the subject to his topic faster than
you can change it back to yours.

*Laurence J. Peter*

Macho does not prove mucho.

*Zsa Zsa Gabor*

Heredity is nothing
      but stored environment.

*Luther Burbank*

Education is the ability to listen
      to almost anything without losing
      your temper or your self-confidence.

*Robert Frost*

Learn your lines
      and don't trip over the furniture.

*Spencer Tracy*

I think that I think; therefore, I think
      that I am.

*Ambrose Bierce*

There's nothing wrong with sound that a little silence won't fix.

*Buster Keaton*

*Observations*

There's right and there's wrong.
You get to do one or the other. You do one
and you're living. You do the other,
and you may be walking around,
but you're dead as a beaver hat.

*John Wayne*


There is nothing so skillful
in its own defense as imperious pride.

*Helen Hunt Jackson*


The only time a woman really succeeds
in changing a man is when he is a baby.

*Natalie Wood*


Write of me not, "Died in bitter pains," but
"Emigrated to another star."

*Helen Hunt Jackson*


A star is somebody who has
a little bit more than somebody else.

*Mae West*

There is more treasure in books than in all
the pirate's loot on Treasure Island.

*Walt Disney*

Give me golf clubs, fresh air and
a beautiful partner, and you can keep
the clubs and the fresh air.

*Jack Benny*

Too many cooks may spoil the broth,
but it only takes one to burn it.

*Julia Child*

Homes really are no more
than the people who live in them.

*Nancy Reagan*

I'm a very good housekeeper.
Whenever I leave a man, I keep his house.

*Zsa Zsa Gabor*

The first rule of politics is to be different.

*Jerry Brown*

Politics is the art of looking for trouble,
finding it everywhere, diagnosing it
incorrectly and applying the wrong remedy.

*Groucho Marx*

Bureaucracy defends the status quo
long past the time when the quo
has lost its status.

*Laurence J. Peter*

The taxpayer is someone who works
for the government but doesn't have to take
a civil-service exam.

*Ronald Reagan*

Government exists to protect us from
each other. We can't afford the government
it takes to protect us from ourselves.

*Ronald Reagan*

Honor is not
the exclusive property
of any political party.

*Herbert Hoover*

Toughness doesn't have to come
in a pinstripe suit.

*Diane Feinstein*

The nine most terrifying words
in the English language are, "I'm from the
government, and I'm here to help."

*Ronald Reagan*

Blessed are the young,
for they shall inherit the national debt.

*Herbert Hoover*

This used to be a government
of checks and balances. Now it's all checks
and no balances.

*Gracie Allen*

The volume of paper expands
     to fill the available briefcase.

*Jerry Brown*


Man is not free unless government
          is limited.

*Ronald Reagan*


Free speech does not live many hours
  after free industry and free commerce die.

*Herbert Hoover*

God is making the world, and the show
is so grand and beautiful and exciting that I
have never been able to study any other.

*John Muir*

The redwoods are ambassadors
from another time.

*John Steinbeck*

Equipped with his five senses,
man explores the universe around him
and calls the adventure science.

*Edwin Hubble*

# Nature is always hinting at us.

*Robert Frost*

It's too bad that all the people who know
how to run the country are busy
driving taxicabs and cutting hair.

*George Burns*

One of the greatest wits of all times
was the person who called them
"Easy Payments."

*George Burns*

You can't cheat an honest man.

*W. C. Fields*

He who hesitates is last.

*Mae West*

The most important thing in acting
is honesty. Once you've learned to fake that,
you've got it made.

*Sam Goldwyn*

About the time we make the ends meet, somebody moves the ends.

*Herbert Hoover*

# Sources

## Sources

Kareem Abdul-Jabbar: 101
Gracie Allen: Entertainer, 152
Woody Allen: Actor, Writer, Director, 138
Walter Alston: Baseball Manager, 44, 54, 55, 77, 104
Fred Astaire: Dancer, 128
Gertrude Atherton: Author, 123, 132
Lucille Ball: Actress, 43, 48, 50, 60, 74, 110, 113, 118, 121
John Barrymore: Actor, Radio Personality, 127
Jack Benny: Entertainer, 65, 128, 149
Ambrose Bierce: San Francisco Journalist, 34, 68, 144, 145, 146
Shirley Temple Black: Santa Monica-born Child Star, 73
Dan Blocker: Actor, 42
Humphrey Bogart: Actor, 106
David Bowie: Entertainer, 136
Tom Bradley: Los Angeles Mayor, 59, 63
Jerry Brown: Governor, 34, 91, 150, 153
James Bryce: 18, 132
Pearl S. Buck: Novelist, 21, 133
Luther Burbank: Horticulturist, 23, 27, 36, 146
George Burns: Entertainer, 47, 52, 57, 110, 111, 114, 142, 156
Raymond Burr: Actor, 50, 73
Jerry Buss: Sports Executive, 100
Herb Caen: 134
Johnny Carson: Entertainer, 42, 45, 101, 110, 129
Jimmy Carter: 39th President of the United States, 32
Raymond Chandler: Writer, 21
Charlie Chaplin: Actor, 26, 67, 122
Cher: Entertainer, 95
Julia Child: Pasadena-born Chef, 53, 118, 149
Chuck Conners: Television Star, 101
Barnaby Conrad: 134
Alistair Cooke: Writer, 24
Norman Cousins: Author, Editor, 52, 66, 82, 88, 126

## Sources

# About the Author

Criswell Freeman is a Doctor of Clinical Psychology living in Nashville, Tennessee. He is the author of *When Life Throws You a Curveball, Hit It* and *The Wisdom Series* from WALNUT GROVE PRESS. He is also a published country music songwriter.

# About Wisdom Books

Wisdom Books chronicle memorable quotations in an easy-to-read style. Written by Criswell Freeman, this series provides inspiring, thoughtful and humorous messages from entertainers, athletes, scientists, politicians, clerics, writers and renegades. Each title focuses on a particular region or special interest.

Combining his passion for quotations with extensive training in psychology, Dr. Freeman revisits timeless themes such as perseverance, courage, love, forgiveness and faith.

"Quotations help us remember the simple yet profound truths that give life perspective and meaning," notes Freeman. "When it comes to life's most important lessons, we can all use gentle reminders."

# The Wisdom Series
*by Dr. Criswell Freeman*

Wisdom Made In America
ISBN 1-887655-07-7

The Book of Southern Wisdom
ISBN 0-9640955-3-X

The Wisdom of the Midwest
ISBN 1-887655-17-4

The Book of Texas Wisdom
ISBN 0-9640955-8-0

The Book of Florida Wisdom
ISBN 0-9640955-9-9

The Book of California Wisdom
ISBN 1-887655-14-X

The Book of New England Wisdom
ISBN 1-887655-15-8

The Book of New York Wisdom
ISBN 1-887655-16-6

The Book of Country Music Wisdom
ISBN 0-9640955-1-3

The Wisdom of Old-Time Television
ISBN 1-887655-64-6

The Golfer's Book of Wisdom
ISBN 0-9640955-6-4

The Wisdom of Southern Football
ISBN 0-9640955-7-2

The Book of Stock Car Wisdom
ISBN 1-887655-12-3

The Wisdom of Old-Time Baseball
ISBN 1-887655-13-1

The Book of Football Wisdom
ISBN 1-887655-18-2